MW01628190

601 West 26th Street, 18th Floor
New York, NY 10001, USA
Tel.: 212 989-6769 Fax: 212 647-0005

**www.assouline.com**



Translated from the French by Elizabeth Too

ISBN: 978 2 75940 305 9

10 9 8 7 6 5 4 3 2

Color separation: Gravor (Switzerland)

Printed by Grafiche Milani (Italy)

# Discovering
# Van Cleef & Arpels

ANNE-MARIE CLAIS

ASSOULINE

Discovering

# Van Cleef & Arpels

A Portrayal of Van Cleef & Arpels inevitably leads to the discovery of a history and imaginative world that have shone brightly in the domain of luxury and design since 1906, the year the House moved into its prestigious Parisian address of 22 Place Vendôme.

The House quickly succeeded in establishing its label as the most desirable of names, and continues to uphold its place in haute jewelry today.

The story begins as most fairy tales end with a heaven sent wedding between Estelle Arpels and Alfred Van Cleef. Estelle is the daughter of a precious stone wholesaler and the sister of two expert gemologists. Alfred is the son of a diamond merchant from Amsterdam. The year is 1896. The die is cast, their adventure will be rich and their relationship fruitful. As in all family stories, Van Cleef & Arpels' has its dark corners. Its world is silent, it knows how to keep secrets, it speaks sotto voce. Trying to unravel it is akin to being initiated into a secret society. To tame the unknown, one must master its language.

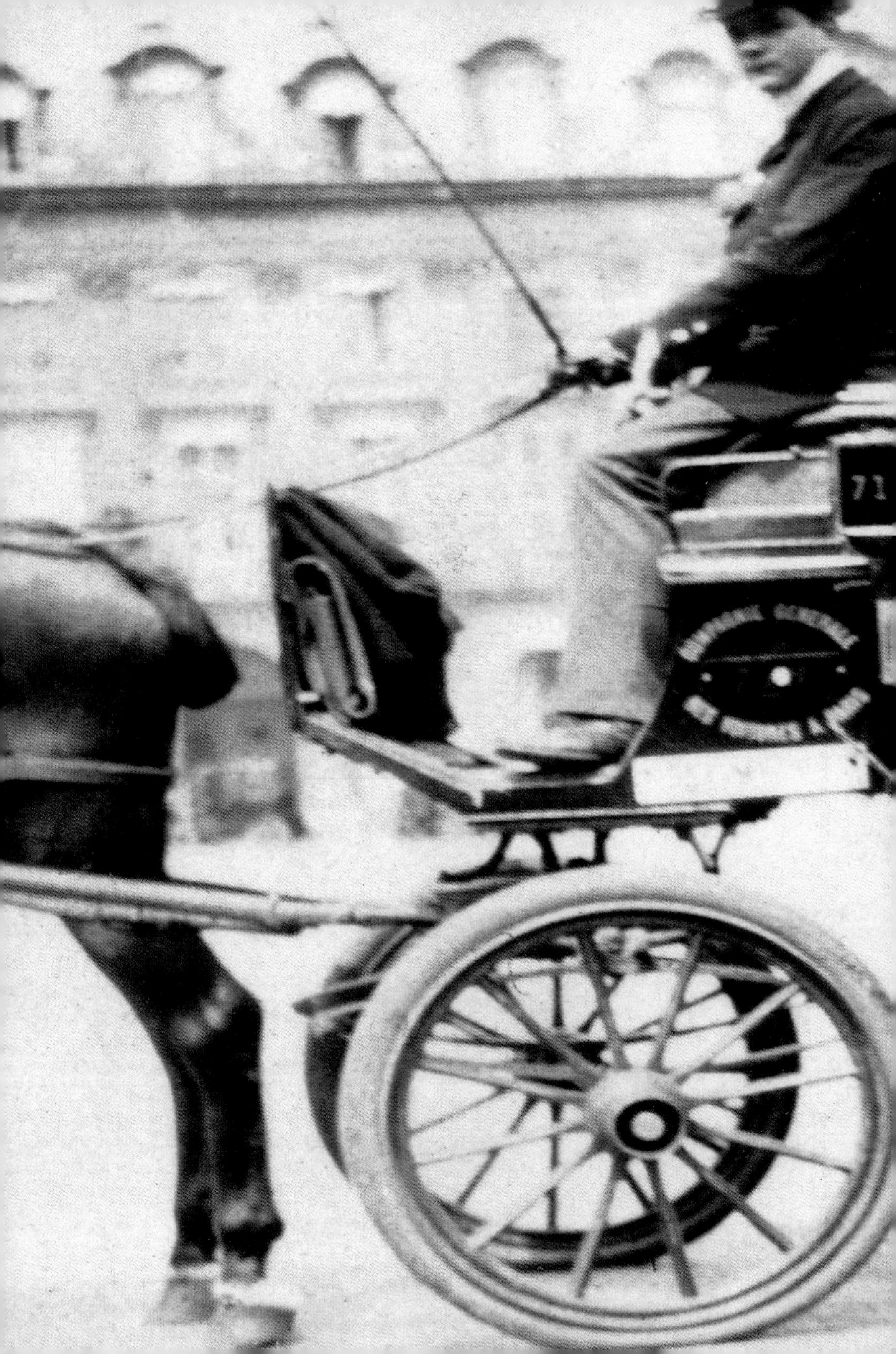
71

# Memory

The Van Cleef & Arpels story is an exceptional one that deserves to be passed down. Its history has been preserved in the House's archives, whose meticulous record keeping reveals how highly valued they are.

It is a whole other kind of precious material: a shared memory that has survived the passage of time. The spirit of the family whose successive generations presided over the House's destiny is alive and well. They all left their mark.

## The Story of a Family...

Shortly after Estelle Arpels and Alfred Van Cleef were married, Alfred became partners with his brothers-in-law, Charles, in 1906, and Julien, in 1908. Louis, the youngest, joined them in 1913.
Each brought his know-how in matters of trade and expertise in precious stones but all had the same drive: to give their best to the building of a brand that went far beyond the importance of a single individual. The union of the two families was of a full and genuine accord: in 1906, registration of the name Van Cleef & Arpels seals their fate. Thus a brand is born, one built on a solid foundation that combined the mastery of a craft with a visionary gift that was to continuously enrich it. That time was one of inventions and dreams. It seemed boundless. In 1909, Louis Blériot was the first to fly over the English Channel in a heavier-than-air machine. This feat symbolized the spirit of adventure that swept over those who saw modernity as a springboard for new ideas. The beginning of the century was marked by innovation. It was the dawn of a new world.

Van Cleef & Arpels was not left unaffected by the spirit of the time. It immediately established its reputation by working exclusively with the highest quality of stones and by pioneering the finest craftsmanship for its settings. This extraordinary attention to detail and passion for the trade will never wane: it is a ceaseless adventure. Stones are sought out on the other side of the world and inspiration is drawn from further still.

Like a declaration of faith, this love for stones is bound up with a love for the trade. Jacques Arpels' keen eye became legendary when he cancelled the sale of the Deepdene at Christie's, a 104-carat daffodil-yellow diamond: while the diamond was natural, its yellow color had been artificially accentuated — something that had not been spotted by gemologists. Stones can hold no secrets from those who love them with passion. They can never lead astray those wise enough to know that Beauty and the Genuine are one and the same.

## A Style That Was to Conquer the World...

But nature is not enough. Exceptional quality stones must be even further refined. In 1926, Alfred Van Cleef's daughter Renée Puissant became Artistic Director and brought an important stylistic momentum that further buttressed the House. Her collaboration with a genius-inspired designer, René Sim Lacaze, infused creations with a definitive impulse that sprang from the stroke of a pencil.

This was the time of graphic modernity, an extension of the movement initiated in architecture by figures such as Walter Gropius and Le Corbusier a few years earlier. Van Cleef & Arpels, however, developed its own style by freeing itself from the fashion and spirit of the moment in a subtle yet assured hand.

The adventure soon went beyond the confines of Place Vendôme to reflect the seasonal lifestyles of the upper class. People were discovering the pleasures of the seaside and embracing the notion of vacation, at a time when the French Riviera was coming of age. Having grasped this phenomenon, Van Cleef & Arpels opened new branches in fashionable seaside resorts and spas: Dinard in 1909, Nice in 1910, Deauville in 1912, Vichy in 1913, and Cannes in 1921 and Monte Carlo in 1935.

WHITE
155·203

VAN CLEEF
&
ARPELS

VAN CLEEF & ARPELS
VAN CLEEF & ARPELS
VAN CLEEF & ARPELS
VAN CLEEF & ARPELS
VAN CLEEF & ARPELS

VAN CLEEF & ARPELS
VAN CLEEF & ARPELS
Van Cleef & Arpels
VAN CLEEF & ARPELS
VAN CLEEF & ARPELS

In 1932 and 1936, Claude and Jacques Arpels joined the company. Pierre Arpels, the youngest member of the second generation, joined them in 1944. Here, we are approaching another crucial turning point in the history of the House. Peril was hovering over Europe and the future was thought to be elsewhere, on the other side of the Atlantic, in America. In 1939, Van Cleef & Arpels opened an office in New York, first at Rockefeller Center, then in 1942 at the address where it still resides today, 744 Fifth Avenue. A Palm Beach branch came into being in 1940.

The sky above Europe darkened. After the storm, life went on: a boutique opened in Dallas, then in Caracas in 1957, and in Beverly Hills in 1969.

The end of the war ushered in the beginning of a new spring. Projects came to fruition in the form of numerous firsts: times had changed and pioneers had new ground to break. Amidst this bustling activity, Van Cleef & Arpels, who in 1954 was the first jeweler to open a "Boutique" in the United States set up shop in Japan in 1974 and presented First in 1976, the first perfume created by a jeweler. Other perfumes were to follow: Van Cleef & Arpels for Men (1978), Gem (1987), Tsar (1988), Van Cleef and Miss Arpels (1993), Zanzibar (2001) and Féerie (2008).

Buoyed up by an incredible energy drawn from the strength of its roots, the House tirelessly expanded its territory. The Boutique des Heures was inaugurated in 1972 to house the new watch designs launched by Pierre Arpels, which included the celebrated PA 49. At last, the time came for opening boutiques in Hong Kong (1982), London (1983 and 1995), Seoul (1990), Moscow (1997), Bal Harbour (2000), and Chicago (2001).

Van Cleef & Arpels became legendary very early on. Its name, which is renowned throughout the world, rests on a solid and highly distinctive reputation: sublime stones, impeccable craftsmanship and a unique style.

These attributes have won it numerous mentions and prizes that duly reward its high standards: the grand prix at the *Exposition Internationale des Arts Décoratifs* in 1925, the grand prix at the *Exposition Coloniale de Paris* in 1931, and it was granted an *hors concours* status at the New York World Fair in 1939. Having been consecrated by honors, the brand reached its zenith in 1992 when the Musée Galliéra did a Van Cleef & Arpels retrospective. This is a name that will undoubtedly leave its mark on history.

## History and Memory...

History affords a glimpse of the family saga through events and important figures that have made this century. The very essence of Van Cleef & Arpels naturally led it to evolve within the highest echelons of society, all brilliantly reflected in its heritage. Its order book contains the most famous names and its creations are associated with the most prestigious occasions. Examples include King Edward VIII's birthday present to Wallis Simpson and the sets of jewels made for the Egyptian princess Fawzia for her marriage to the shah of Iran in 1938. In 1955, Prince Rainier of Monaco chose a pearl and round diamond set as his engagement present to Grace Kelly and appointed the House as official purveyor to the Principality of Monaco.

In 1967, Van Cleef & Arpels was commissioned to design a crown and set of jewels for the coronation of Farah Palhavi as the Empress of Iran. It turned out to be one of the House's most celebrated creations. The precious stones that were to be used had to remain within the confines of the fabulous Tehran Treasure Hall; in fact, it took no less than twenty-four trips for Pierre Arpels to finalize the details of its composition.

112

Paris, le 22 Mai 1939 112

| N° | Désignation | M Dsse de Windsor | 236. |
|---|---|---|---|
| 236 | 1 Collerette b.ts rubis. faire collier selon dessin et instr. Mr W. | | |
| | | collerette brillants et rubis. | |
| | | lot 713. 19 rubis 26.10 x 1416. | 36 957 |
| | | 6 . 5.67 x 1416. | 8028 |
| | fin Juin | 7 . 6.15 x 1770 | 10885 |
| | | facture Sterlé. 148 bag. 13.91 x 3105 | 43.190 |
| | | 14 bts 0.39 x 2000 | 780 |
| | | Relittage des rubis | 1.885 |
| | | Monture | 41.200 |
| | | | 142.925 |
| | | 10% | 14292 |
| | | | 157.217 | 157.217 |

…cliente et de nos lots il y a sur la collerette
44 rubis 224.57
60 bagtes 30.44
14 bts 0.39

du lot 713 { 19 Rubis 26.10 × 8… / 6 " 5.67 × 8… / 7 " 6.15 × 1…

à la cliente { 112 " 186.65 / 112 Baguettes 16.53

The story of Van Cleef & Arpels is unmistakably a love story. Marriages and engagements provide abundant and happy opportunities for the House to maintain a close relationship to the royal courts of Europe and around the world. A Van Cleef & Arpels jewel is above all a promise of happiness.

This special relationship with royalty will never wane. Throughout time, it actually enabled numerous acquisitions. That is how the House came to possess the diadems of Empress Josephine in 1940, Marie of Serbia (whose diadem belonged to the Romanov family) in 1949 and Empress Marie-Louise in 1953.
These historical pieces from European dynasties have provided inspiration for Van Cleef & Arpels jewels designed for the heirs of other prominent families, those who have survived the turmoil of the past century and with whom the House still maintains a privileged relationship.

All this did not come about by chance. Van Cleef & Arpels secured its place in this very exclusive world of haute jewelry when it moved into Place Vendôme in 1906. That moment is not without significance; the brand was on the verge of meeting its destiny.
Blending elegance and whimsy, and defining the essence of the French soul, the House draws upon the Right Bank and the Faubourg Saint Honoré for inspiration to bring that soul to life. We are at the turn of the century and something extraordinary is in the making.

## History Has Its Reasons...

Place Vendôme is the French spirit incarnate. Nurtured by influences of that grand monarchical seventeenth century, this spirit laid the foundations of Classicism: harmony, simplicity, elegance and balance.

These principles were expressed not only through architecture, but also through various art forms, painting, gardens, sculpture, etc.
At that very moment, Classicism evolved beyond limits brought about by the French Revolution and beyond the aristocratic context in which it was born, far away from Faubourg Saint-Germain. Indeed its most fervent believers were not its legitimate heirs.
This quest for recognition began in the nineteenth century with the instigation of the First and Second Empire aristocracies as well as new bourgeois, industrial, and financial dynasties, amongst which prominent Jewish families played an important role.
The figureheads involved in this pursuit of tradition are Count Moïse de Camondo, whose mansion in Plaine Monceau epitomises this French spirit, and Marcel Proust who was its brilliant and faithful chronicler.

It is within this context that we must place Van Cleef & Arpels, as more inclined to strengthen bonds than to break them. At the Place Vendôme, the brand finds its permanent home in a place of culture teeming with history, a place where a new world is about to be born.
This is the world of luxury — a new term that was to transform the Right Bank into a place of light, permanently graced by springtime. As the American magazine *Flair* eloquently put it in 1950: "April touches the Place Vendôme." The House was to become an integral element to this unfolding history of luxury, and so fulfill its destiny.

## The Role of the Arts...

For Van Cleef & Arpels, creative seasons follow one after another, filled with culture and history, and drawing inspiration from its extraordinary collaborations with major figures in the arts. In 1962, Marc Chagall designs a rooster brooch in its studios. In the sixties,

Claude Arpels befriends choreographer George Balanchine in New York and together they conceive a ballet. The Jeweler lends its name to the literary world when it makes the Academician's swords of Alphonse-Pierre Juin (1953), Bernard Gavoty (1976), Mstislav Rostropovitch (1988), and Jeanne Moreau's brooch (2001) on the occasion of their appointment to the Académie Française. In 1997, Van Cleef & Arpels collaborates with the designer Jean-Paul Gaultier by having his haute couture models wear the House's latest creations. Indeed, Van Cleef & Arpels has a flair for orchestrating fruitful encounters and uniting different art forms.

## A Story of Creation...

Van Cleef & Arpels never ceases to innovate. From the drafting studio to the fabrication workshops, curiosity is its passionate driving force. For it is not enough to simply feed off a legacy, no matter how illustrious it may be; it is necessary to make one's contribution to the development of the brand.

Made in 1930, the Minaudière was one such creation. As the story goes, one day Charles Arpels caught Florence Jay Gould slipping her lipstick into a white tin box.
Without further ado, the Minaudière was born, taking after a secret drawer or magician's box so that the well-bred woman could tuck away her handkerchief and powder puff without becoming encumbered.
This invention, a true technical feat that succeeds in capturing infinite femininity within a minuscule object, a precursor of the vanity case, is patented and registered as a trademark. Unfolding to reveal various purse accessories inlaid with landscapes, flowers, or chinoiseries, it bears sophisticated refinements worthy of exquisite eighteenth-century furniture.

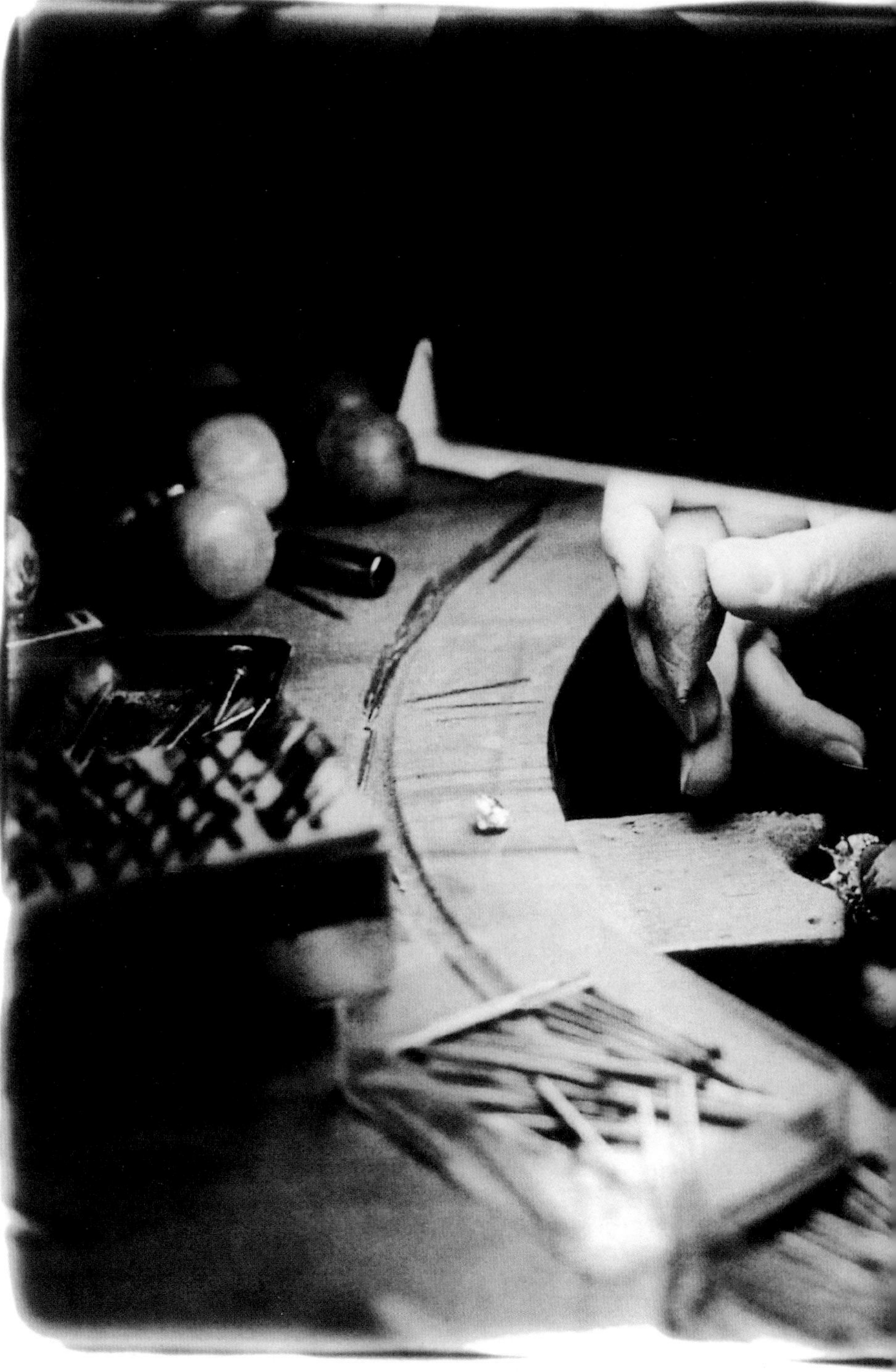

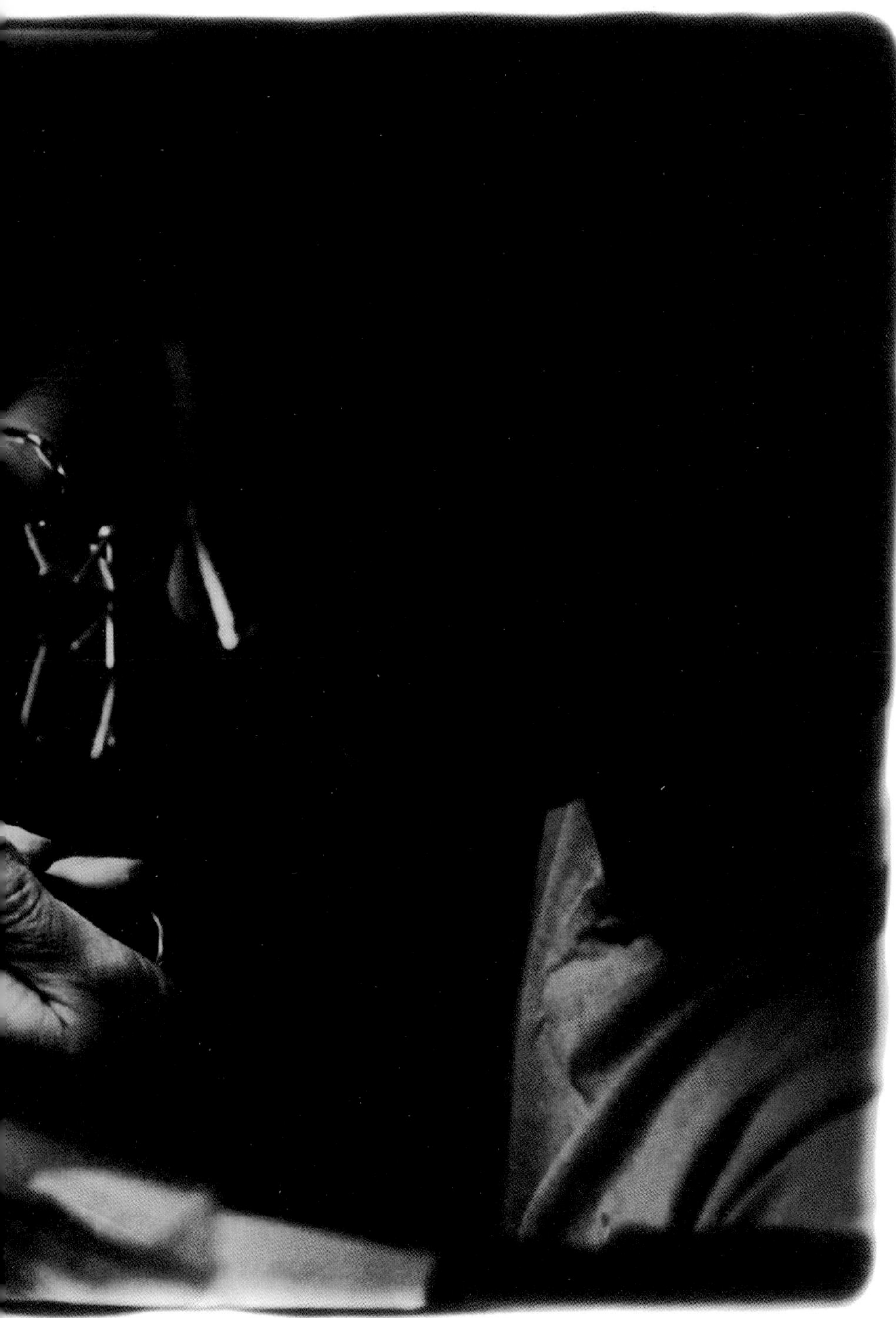

Another element of paramount importance to Van Cleef & Arpels's reputation is the invention of the Mystery Setting in 1933. This extremely ingenious technique, which consists of settings devoid of any visible prongs, graces numerous forms with its stunning simplicity: bracelets, brooches with floral or butterfly patterns, Boule rings, etc.

This unique process, built on a know-how covetously safeguarded over time, continues to distinguish the House today. It is extremely labor intensive: no less than 90 hours per ring, approximately 300 hours for a brooch, and up to 1,400 hours for the famous Clip du Millénaire, which was presented at the *Biennale des Antiquaires* in the year 2000. The Mystery Setting transcends matter itself and celebrates design: it comes to life and it is fed by light. The Ludo bracelet of 1933 is one such example. The master craftsman's magic fashions gold into intricate honeycomb patterns. Like the stone, the metal now softens and becomes malleable, almost alive.

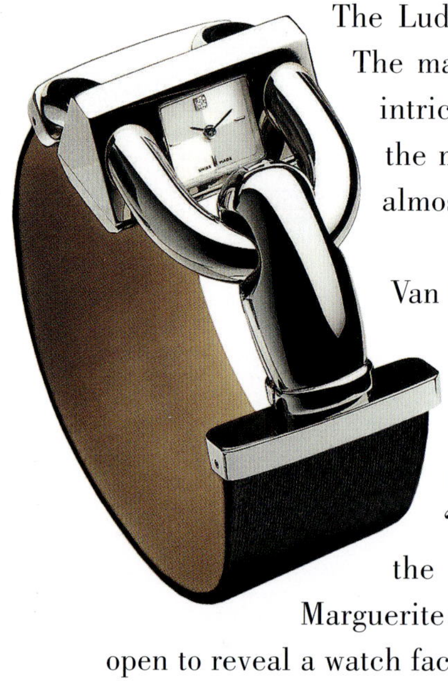

Van Cleef & Arpels never ceased to participate in renewing the tradition of the craft and its history has become inseparable from that of jewelry design. As early as the twenties, watches were transformed into "jewels that tell the time." This idea was the basis of many creations, such as the Marguerite brooch, whose precious stone center flips open to reveal a watch face. Out of that same concern for functionality and desire to combine the useful with the beautiful, the famous Cadenas watch-bracelet is created in 1935.

The past sparks designs that become a focal point for influences that are continually revisited. Van Cleef & Arpels has the gift of memory.

Its sense of style draws upon the rich history of the Decorative Arts: Mystery Setting mosaics or the Ludo, newly-adapted Egyptian styles inspired by the discoveries of Howard Carter and Lord Carnarvon in the Tomb of Tutankhamen in 1922, Second Empire designs, chinoiseries, and Japanism.

The Jeweler also pays attention to the art of textile and fashion, envisioning precious materials as noble substances to be worked like fabric or twisting metal like a fiber, thus creating knots, weaves, cords, drops, tassels and other decorative details. The same technique applies to  stones. Precious metal becomes lace, tulle and nets.

The House's true talent lies in its unerring ability to discern and incorporate new influences so as to better mold them and to revitalize its distinct historical vernacular. As Giuseppe Tomasi di Lampedusa puts it: "If we want things to stay the same, things will have to change."

CLEEF
5th AVENUE
& ARPELS INC.
NEW YORK

# An Imaginative World

The Van Cleef & Arpels story is steeped in an imaginative world. The House will never forget that it owes its name to two families who were faced with migration and exile, and for whom continuity was not a material concern but a question of loyalty, of respect for a legacy and its values. Time may be elusive and ever changing, but the world nonetheless constantly repeats itself.

With a curiosity fueled by many influences and a passion for minutiae embedded in its creations, Van Cleef & Arpels has always revered the past. Whether it features an inlaid floral pattern that harks back to precious eighteenth-century furniture, or cherry tree blossoms adorning the lid of a Minaudière as if borrowed from some piece of Japanese lacquer-ware, or an Egyptian frieze unfolding as a bracelet — every object evokes a story.

## Capturing Nature in Movement

Van Cleef & Arpels strives to capture the cyclical movements of nature at its most beautiful instant — when nature's vital force and its intense fragility bloom simultaneously.

Every flower speaks to its beholder: the Pivoine (1937-1974) and Rose brooches bring to mind a fragrance, or entice the hand to softly caress them. The Hirondelle (1938) or Papillon brooch seems to fly off with a quiet whisper of wings. The Mouchoir pattern appears to crease under fingers barely touching it. The Éléments are the lifeblood of this enchanted world: water trickles in rivers of diamonds or freezes into fragile crystals of snow; fire dances in the Flamme brooch (1934); and wind blows on precious stone bouquets (Bouquet Brooch, 1940), bending their stems and transcribing its movement upon them. And everywhere, the Mysterious Setting continues to successfully conceal its hand: it fills the gaze with wonder and begs to be touched, but it never reveals anything about its inner secrets.

A Van Cleef & Arpels creation is a permanent invitation to the awakening of the senses and desire. Its view of the world is sensory and organic; it is a world that continually renews itself without ever changing.

## Transcending Matter

Thus re-created for us, this natural state demands an extraordinary mastery of materials. The trick is to never make this astonishing skill apparent, but rather to always transcend it in order to leave behind an impression of ineffable grace. Van Cleef & Arpels creations are founded upon complex architectures that are patiently elaborated in the secrecy

of the jeweler's studios. Based on drawings and transformed by technical skill, its clever constructions are numerous.

When Van Cleef & Arpels celebrates nature, its aim is to capture and tame all that is fluid and ephemeral. Asymmetry becomes a natural byproduct thereby ensuring a timeless sense of flow. Moreover, the House imposed its own sense of style. In the forties, everyone gives in to the temptation of the monumental. Van Cleef & Arpels goes further and makes lightness a sophisticated principle of subversion. Volutes become softly articulated (the 1938 necklace with cabochon emeralds and baguette diamonds set in platinum) while the Jeweler's style asserts itself by magically relie-ving matter of its excess weight. That is how the Alvéoles bracelet (1947) was created, one whose sophisticated links take nothing away from its remarkable harmony.
Even when it comes to more imposing pieces, form and emphasis on detail have always prevailed.
This craftsmanship can almost be likened to alchemy where deep forces breathe life into metal and stone, and the object itself. For it is truly a life-force that inhabits this House, an ever changing organic thrust. The most spectacular example must be the transformable Passe-Partout

VAN CLEEF
ARPELS
PARIS

jewel. Created in 1939, this rare and versatile object enables its owner, on a whim, to wear it as a belt, a brooch, or as pendants. This exceptionally modern invention has since been a constant source of inspiration: the latest creation, the Bijou Cadenas (2000) can equally clasp a throat, belt a waist, or adorn a wrist. It offers numerous facets to the unique woman who is always ready to defy conventions.
Likewise, by juxtaposing transparency with opacity, Van Cleef & Arpels celebrates a perpetually shifting state of mind, much like that of a woman who loves to seduce. This game of contrast is multifaceted. Jewelry adorns the body the same way clothing can. The Zip necklace can, according to one's mood, be worn open or closed; a net of gold can hide or reveal . . . The intimate relationship between a woman and a jewel is unconditional; they become accomplices.

## The Eternal Feminine

The Van Cleef & Arpels woman is imbued with a sophisticated charm that makes her at once fascinating, timeless and desirable. One word sums it up: Glamour.

This is the case for all the admirers of the House, including Elizabeth Taylor, Sophia Loren, Jeanne Moreau, Audrey Hepburn, Florence Jay Gould, Maria Callas, Marlene Dietrich, Joan Fontaine, Michèle Morgan, Gloria Swanson, Ludmilla Tcherina, Romy Schneider, Isabelle Adjani, Sharon Stone, Noor de Jordanie and Lady Diana.
While Van Cleef & Arpels has won the heart of women, it has rarely cast her image in its creations. The dancer is one of the only female representations in its repertoire. Whether or not she has wings, like the Spirit of Beauty brooch, she is always endowed with the power of metamorphosis that is characteristic of many other Van Cleef & Arpels jewels.

Indeed, this theme of dance is not without significance. The spirit underlying a century of history and creation was encapsulated in a single ballet. Conceived by Claude Arpels and George Balanchine in 1961, this ballet is entitled Jewels and its first performance took place in 1967. It is arguably considered the first ballet with three scenes. Like the choreographer who participated in the great saga of Russian ballet and in revolutionizing dance in the twentieth century, Jewels proclaims its innovative nature. In 2007, the full-length version of the ballet Jewels was staged by the Royal Opera House in London. For this occasion, Van Cleef & Arpels created the High Jewellery collection "Ballet Précieux" presented in homage to the exceptional encounter between choreographer and jeweller. The entire world of Van Cleef & Arpels is contained in these three scenes.

With music by Gabriel-Urbain Fauré, the first one represents France. It speaks of youth, freshness, and spontaneity. It is the bearer of tradition of a kind of classicism born to be re-invented. Its color is emerald green, the color of springtime.

With a jazz-like theme by Igor Stravinsky, the second scene represents New York, America, the New World, and its energy, vitality and creative momentum. Its color is ruby red. It is the blood of life, the celebration of modernity. The whole future of the House is expressed in a single color.

Lastly, the third scene, with a musical score by Pyotr Tchaikovsky, honors the memory of Old Europe and Imperial Russia. It expresses a romantic ideal built on dreams and desires. Its color is the snow white of diamonds.

And thus the imaginary landscape of the House is mapped out around two cardinal points: East and West.

# Style

Van Cleef & Arpels has always maintained a style that transcends its history and fuels its imagination. It is timeless, like the woman the brand is designed for; her silhouette, toned and subtle, is endowed with a youthfulness capable of renewing itself and upon which time never seems to have any effect.

# Nature

*The language of flowers is*
*as old as the world itself,*
*yet it never ages*
*because it is reborn every spring.*

Charlotte de La Tour

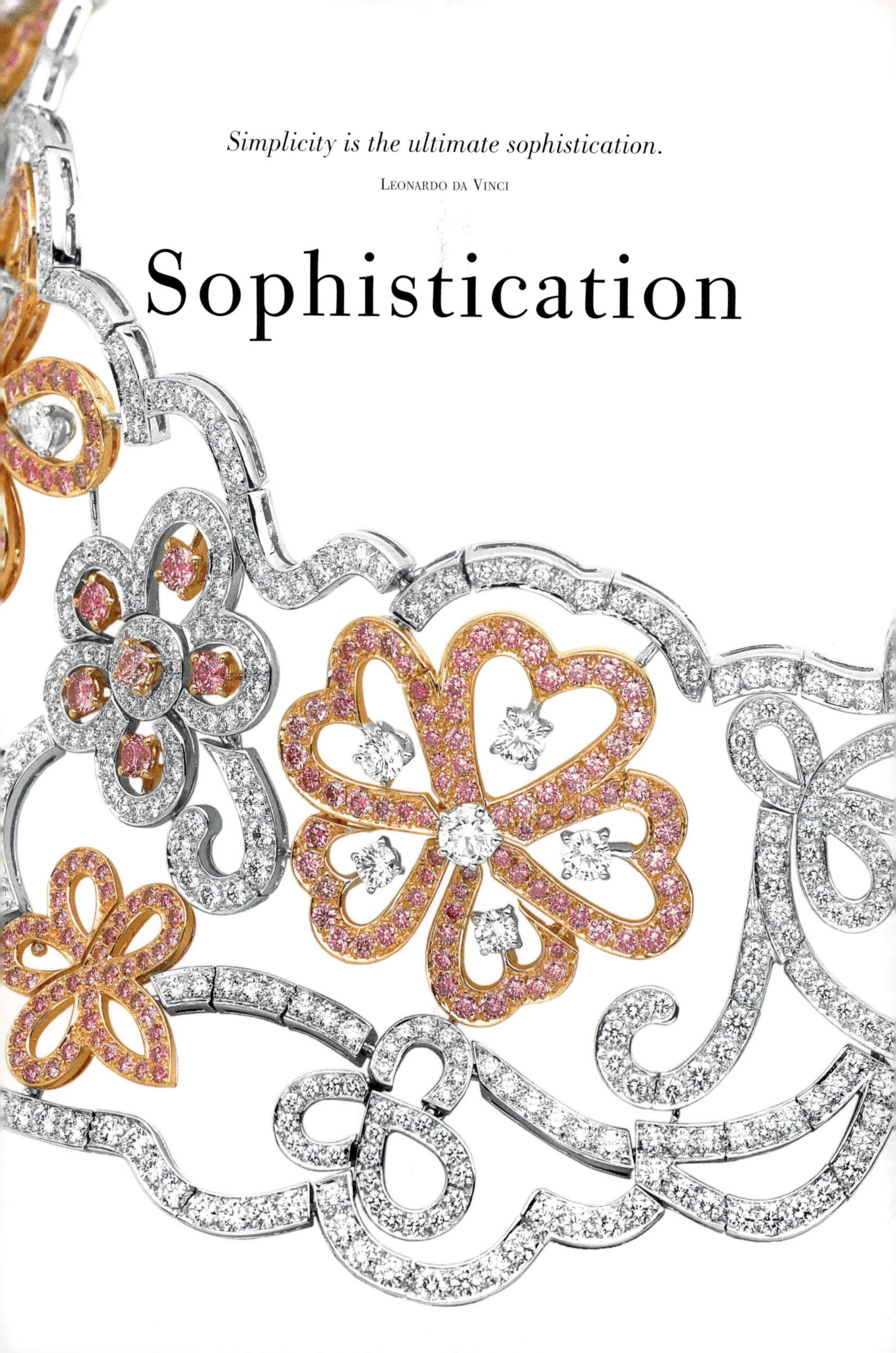

*Simplicity is the ultimate sophistication.*

Leonardo da Vinci

# Sophistication

# Femininity

*I don't mind living in a man's world as long as I can be a woman in it.*

Marilyn Monroe

# Metamorphosis

*The world of art belongs to the realm of metamorphosis,*
*not immortality.*

André Malraux

Van Cleef & Arpels
SWISS
MADE

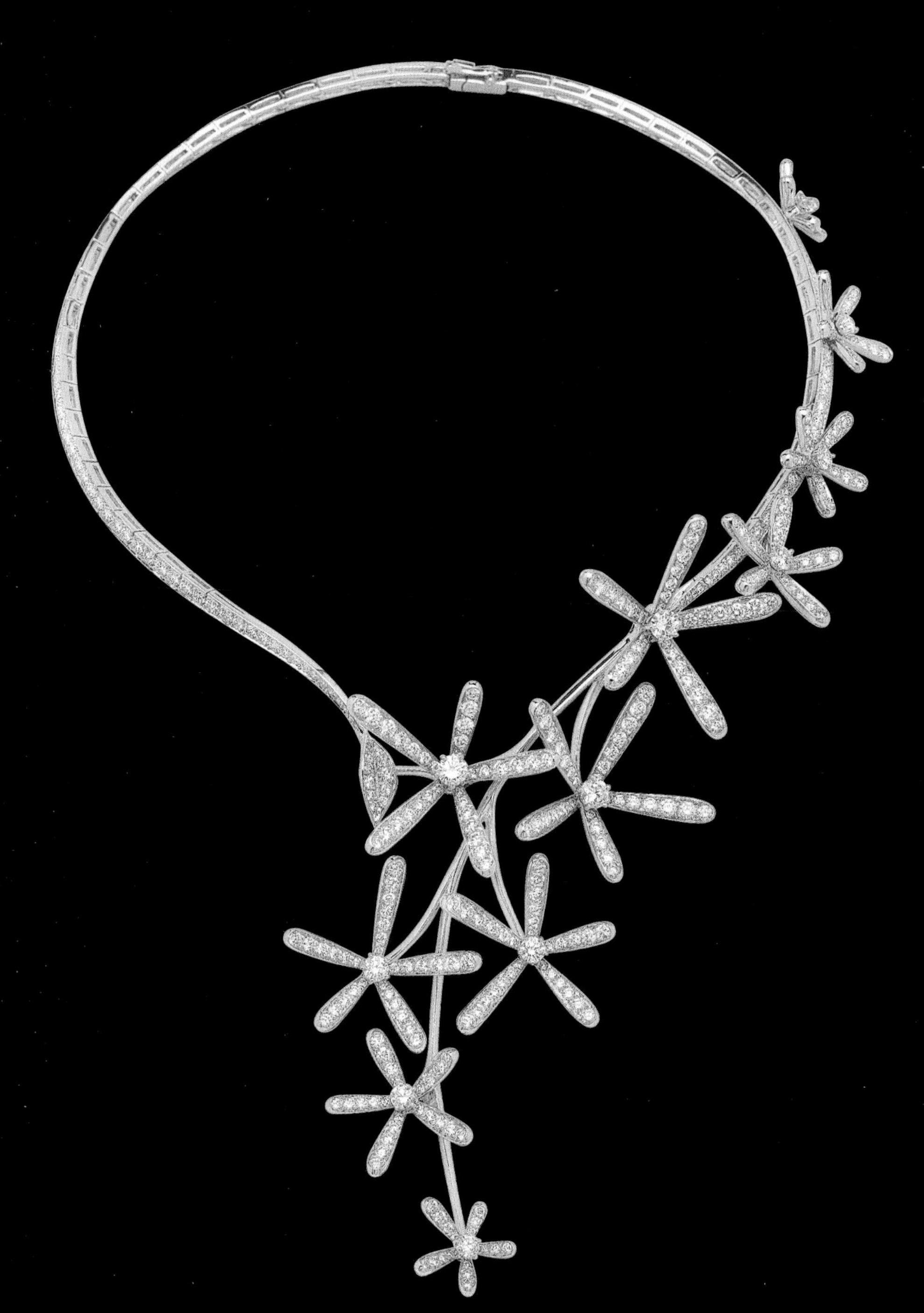

# Glamour

*Something indefinite, inaccessible to normal women, an unreal paradise, desirable but basically out of reach.*

Marlene Dietrich

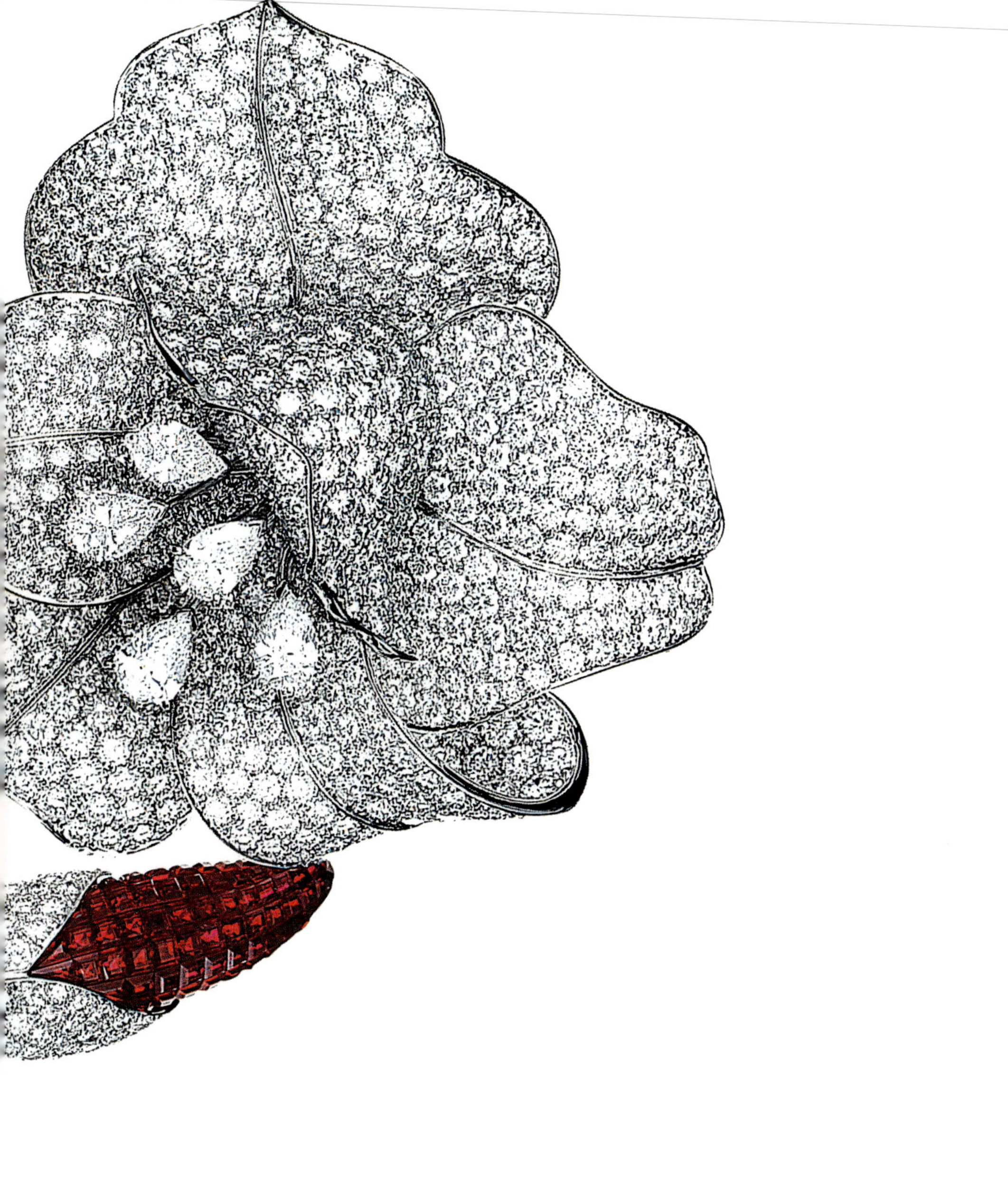

VAN CLEEF
&ARPELS
SWISS MADE

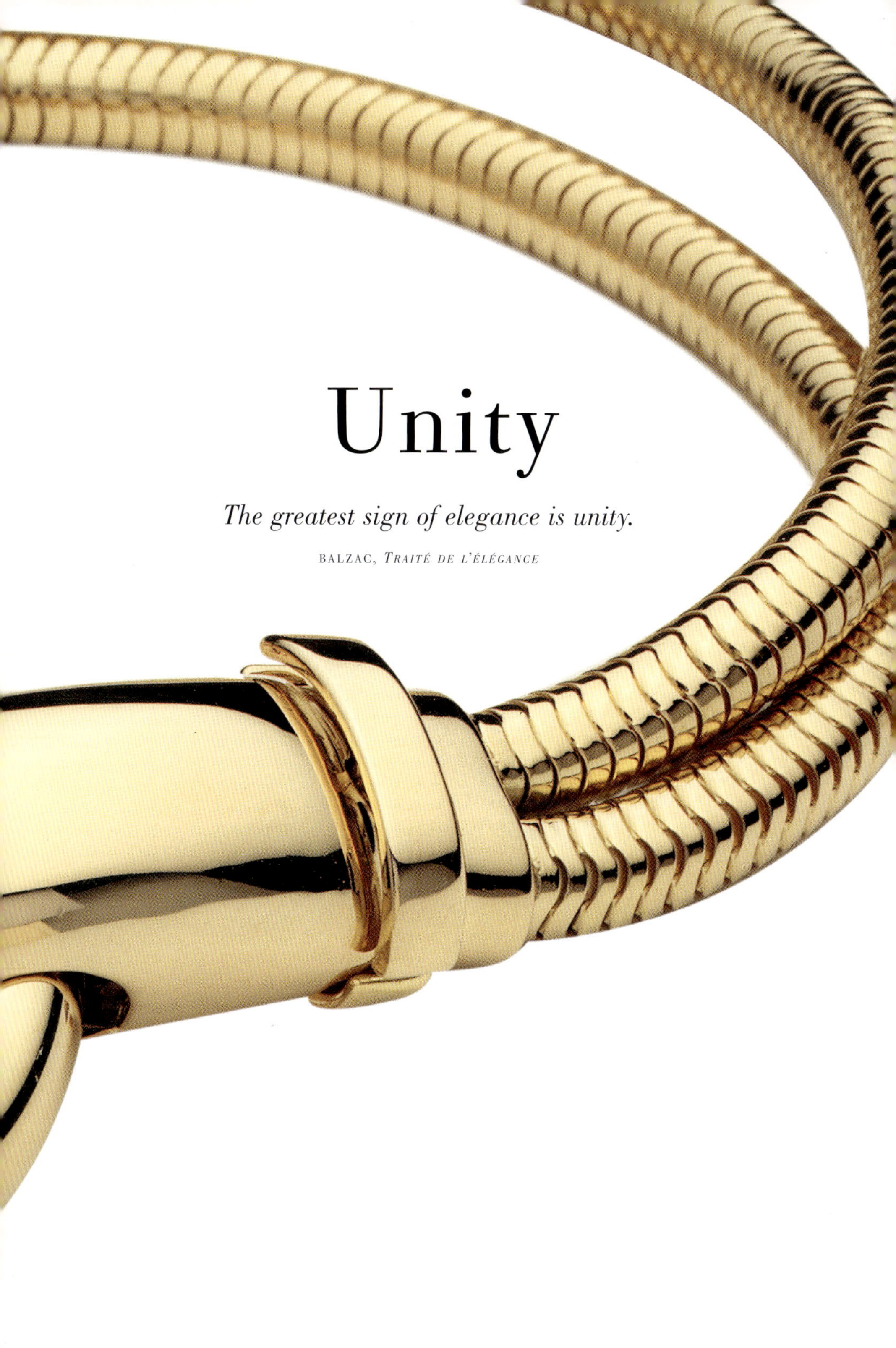

# Unity

*The greatest sign of elegance is unity.*

BALZAC, *TRAITÉ DE L'ÉLÉGANCE*

# Simplicity

*The secret to elegance is to look like oneself.*

HUBERT DE GIVENCHY

# Milestones

# The History of a Great Name

1894 Léon Arpels, a precious stone merchant, moves into 34 rue Drouot, in Paris.

1896 His daughter, Estelle, marries Alfred Van Cleef, the son of a diamond merchant.

1906 Alfred and his brother-in-law, Charles, register the name "Van Cleef & Arpels." The boutique settles into 22 Place Vendôme.

1908 Julien Arpels becomes partners with his brother and brother-in-law.

1909 Opening of a new branch in Dinard.

1910 Opening of a new branch in Nice.

1912 Opening of a new branch in Deauville.

1913 Opening of a new branch in Vichy. Louis Arpels joins the company.

1917 Patent granted by His Royal Highness Prince Don Antonio of Orléans.

1919 Opening of a new branch in Lyons.

1921 Opening of a new branch in Cannes.

1925 Grand prix at the *Exposition Internationale des Arts Décoratifs.*

1926 Renée Puissant, daughter of Alfred Van Cleef, becomes Artistic Director. Beginning of her collaboration with the designer René Sim Lacaze.

1927 Opening of a new branch in Touquet-Plage.

1929 Takes part in Exposition de Joaillerie et Orfèvrerie at the Palais Galliéra. Opening of an office in New York.

1931 Grand prix at the Exposition Coloniale de Paris.

1932 Julien's eldest son, Claude, joins the company.

1933 Opening of a new branch in Roubaix.

1935 Opening of a boutique in the Garnier Casino-Opera in Monte Carlo. The V.C.A. hallmark enters the *Annuaire azur.*

1936 Jacques Arpels, Julien's second son, joins the company. King Edward VIII, the former Prince of Wales, gives Wallis Simpson a Van Cleef & Arpels ruby and diamond set on her fortieth birthday.

1937 The Duke of Windsor gives Mrs. Simpson the famous Jarretière bracelet and brooch made of sapphires in Mystery Setting on the occasion of their wedding. Takes part in the 1937 World Expo.

1938 Death of Alfred Van Cleef. Designs jewelry sets for Princess Fawzia, the sister of King Farouk of Egypt, for her marriage to the Shah of Iran.

## The History of a Great Name

1939 Honored with an hors concours status at the New York World Fair.
Opening of an office in New York, at the Rockefeller Center.

1940 Opening of a branch in Palm Beach.
Acquisition of Empress Josephine's tiara given by Napoleon on the occasion of their marriage.

1942 Death of Renée Puissant. Van Cleef & Arpels moves into 744 Fifth Avenue in New York, where it still resides today.

1944 Pierre Arpels, the youngest member of the second generation, enters the company.

1945 Takes part in the exhibition Le Petit Théâtre de la Mode in Paris.

1949 Acquisition of Marie of Serbia's diadem (which belonged to the Romanov family).

1951 Takes part in the bi-millennial celebrations in Paris. Death of Charles Arpels.

1953 Acquisition of Empress Marie-Louise's diadem and the Cœur Bleu, a 30.82-carat diamond. Designs Marshal Juin's academician's sword.

1954 Inauguration of the very first jeweler's "Boutique."

1955 Prince Rainier III chooses a Van Cleef & Arpels pearl and diamond parure for his fiancée Grace Kelly. The House becomes the official purveyor of the Principality of Monaco.

1956 In Bombay, Claude Arpels buys the 114-carat diamond known as the Blue Princess or Neele Ranee, and it is subsequently sold to Florence Jay Gould.

1957 Opening of a boutique in Caracas.

1960 Opening of a boutique in Geneva. In London, Jacques Arpels buys the Princie Diamond, a 34.64-carat pink diamond.

1961 The catch phrase "Il est des signatures auxquelles on tient" is registered.

1964 Death of Julien Arpels. Designs a necklace for Queen Sirikit of Thailand for the wedding of Anne-Marie and Constantine of Greece.

1967 Designs Farah Pahlavi's coronation crown and necklace.

1969 Opening of a branch in Beverly Hills.

1971 Acquisition of the Briolette, a 95-carat pear-yellow diamond, and the Thibaw, a 26.13-carat Burmese ruby named after the king of Burma.

1972 Inauguration of the Boutique des Heures, Place Vendôme.

1974 First French jeweler to set up shop in Japan.
Designs the academician's swords of Jean-Jacques Gautier and André Roussin.

1975 Registration of the trademark First.

1976 Launching of the perfume First, the first fragrance signed by a jeweler.
Designs Bernard Gavoty's academician's sword.

1978 Grace of Monaco wears the 17-pear-diamond tiara for the wedding of Princess Caroline. Launching of the eau de toilette Van Cleef & Arpels for Men.

## The History of a Great Name

1980 Death of Pierre Arpels.

1982 Opening of a sales outlet in Hong Kong.

1983 Opening of a boutique in London.

1985 Rainier III presides over the fiftieth anniversary of the boutique in his Principality. Takes part in the exhibition L'Art de Vivre en France in Tokyo.

1987 Launching of the perfume Gem. First museum presentation in Tokyo.

1988 Designs Mstislav Rostropovitch's academician's sword.
The men's perfume Tsar is launched in St. Petersburg.

1989 Takes part in the exhibition L'Art de Vivre en France in New York.

1990 Death of Claude Arpels. First retrospective in the United States: The Artistry of Van Cleef & Arpels. Shown in Los Angeles, Washington, and Honolulu (1991).
Opening of a boutique in Seoul.

1992 Van Cleef & Arpels retrospective at the Musée de la Mode et du Costume, Palais Galliéra.

1993 Launching of two perfumes: Van Cleef and Miss Arpels.

1994 First French jeweler to set up shop in Shanghai.

1995 Opening of a salon at Harrods in London.

1996 Centennial of Alfred Van Cleef and Estelle Arpels's marriage.
Inauguration of the renovated Place Vendôme salons, sponsored by Sharon Stone

1997 Opening of a boutique in Moscow. Retrospective in Tokyo.
Participates in the "First" summer ball for Monaco's 700th birthday.
Participation in the Jean-Paul Gaultier fashion show.

1999 Groupe Richemont takes a stake in Van Cleef & Arpels.
Launching of the perfume Birmane.

2000 Opening of a boutique in rue du Faubourg Saint-Honoré in Paris and in Miami (Bal Harbour USA).

2001 Launching of Zanzibar, perfume for men.
Creation of Jeanne Moreau's academician's brooch.
Opening of new branches in Moscow, Taipei, Osaka, Chicago and Hawaii.
Creation of the new boutique concept by Anoushka Hempel and first openings in Monaco, Tokyo and Palm Beach.

2002 Opening of new boutiques in Geneva, Saint Moritz, Singapore, Hong Kong (Prince's Building), Taipei (Regent Galleria), Osaka, Tokyo (Ikebukuro Seibu), Yokohama (Sogo), Seoul (Hyundai Main) and Costa Mesa (South Cost Plaza).

2003 Participation in the Victor&Rolf fashion show, Spring/Summer 2003-2004.
The opening of boutiques in Tokyo (Isetan Shinjuku), Nagoya, Americana Manhasset.

# The History of a Great Name

2004 Participation in the Lagerfeld Gallery fashion show, Autumn/Winter 2004-2005.
Exhibition of Van Cleef & Arpels jewellery in the permanent collection of the Jewellery Gallery of the Museum of Decorative Arts, Paris.
Opening of boutiques in London (New Bond Street), Paris (Printemps du Luxe), Athens, Yekaterinburg, Dubai, Hong Kong (Pacific Place), Fukuoka, Tokyo (Mitsukoshi Nihonbashi) and Montreal.

2005 Participation in the Lagerfeld Gallery fashion show, Autumn/Winter 2005-2006.
Opening of stores in Lisbon, Athens, Moscow (Stoleshnikov ul.) Kiev, Almaty, Flagship in Tokyo (Ginza), Beijing, Taipei (Taipei 101), Seoul (Lotte "Avenuel").
Publication of the book *Reflets d'Éternité* at Cercle d'Art Publishing.

2006 Celebration of the hundredth anniversary of Van Cleef & Arpels: "A century of glamour and excellence".
Opening of boutiques in Shanghai, Abu Dhabi, Hong Kong, Istanbul and Chiba.
Re-opening of the salons at 22, place Vendôme in Paris, redesigned by Patrick Jouin.
The publication of Visionnaire no. 48 "Magic" devoted to Van Cleef & Arpels.
Participation at the Rodarte fashion show in New York. Spring/ Summer 2006-2007.
Launch of the perfume First Love.

2007 Opening of stores in Seoul, Kuala Lumpur, Singapore, Beijing, Moscow, Riyadh, and Nagoya.
Retrospective of former and contemporary designs in Tokyo and Osaka.
Participation in the exhibition "The Story of Tiara" in Tokyo, Niigata and Kyoto.
Participation in the Lanvin fashion show in Paris and the Rodarte fashion show in New York. Autumn/Winter 2007-2008.

2008 Opening of stores in Cannes, Dubaï, Macau, Sendei and Las Vegas.
Participation in the Haute Couture fashion show of the designer Eymeric François in Paris.
Death of Jacques Arpels.
Retrospective of former and contemporary designs in Seoul.
Participation in the American International Fine Art Fair in Palm Beach, World Fine Art in Moscow and La Biennale des Antiquaires in Paris.
Design of an engagement ring in partnership with Alber Elbaz for Lanvin.
Design of a jewelled evening bag in partnership with Chloe, a limited edition intended for Japan.
Launch of the Haute Parfumerie Féerie fragrance.

2009 Opening of stores in Milan, Seoul, Busan, Hong Kong (MPS), Beijing Wang Fu Jing, Naples (Florida) and Honolulu.
The Art of Magical Jewels exhibition, Art Dubaï.
The Spirit of Beauty exhibition at the Mori Arts Center of Tokyo.
Launch of the "Collection Extraordinaire": six Haute Parfumerie fragrances.
Publication of the book *Le Temps poétique* at Cercle d'Art Publishing.

# The History of a style

1916 Wooden jewelry.

1918 Van Cleef & Arpels creates the first châtelaine, a jewel that is worn at the waist with a watch fastened to it.

1922 Oiseau brooch, which could be worn as a feathered hat pin.

1923 Art Deco Entrelacs brooch. Art Deco Bow brooch.

1924 Brooch–belt buckle of Egyptian inspiration.
Jewel of Chinese inspiration.
Launching of brooches in the form of bow ties.

1925 Wide Indian-style "manchette" bracelet.
The Van Cleef & Arpels brooch representing blooming roses takes the grand prix at the Exposition Internationale des Arts Décoratifs in Paris.

1927 Plume brooch.

1928 Hirondelle brooch.

1930 Charles Arpels's design for the Minaudière is inspired by Florence Jay Gould.

1932 The new metal alloy Styptor becomes a registered trademark.

1933 Invention of the Mystery Setting. Ludo bracelet, which can be taken apart.

1934 Flamme brooch.

1935 The first Boule ring, rubies or sapphires in Mystery Setting. Trèfle jewel.

1936 Cadenas watch-bracelet.

1938 The versatile Bijou Cadenas is patented.

1939 Passe-Partout becomes a registered trademark.
The Zip necklace design is inspired by the Duchess of Windsor but it must wait until 1951 before it is fabricated.
Coffre ring, topped by a domed motif.

1942 Danseuse brooch. Tulle jewel.

1943 La Fourragère becomes a registered trademark.

1946 Fraise necklace. Pochette brooch, also known as the Coin de Mouchoir.

1948 Jewels inspired by Peter Pan collars.

1949 Pierre Arpels designs the PA 49 watch, which has a round ultra-flat casing.

1950 Ballerine necklace. Chantilly ring.

1952 Macramé jewel.

## The History of a style

| | |
|---|---|
| 1958 | Zodiac Charms (Boutique). |
| 1962 | Chagall designs clip Coq brooch in Van Cleef & Arpels studios.<br>Lion Mane jewel. |
| 1963 | Twist ring. |
| 1964 | Bébé Lion jewel. |
| 1967 | *Jewels*, the three-act ballet conceived by Balanchine and Claude Arpels, premières in New York. |
| 1968 | Chevalerie Chain. Philippines ring. |
| 1972 | Modèle Valette version, inspired by the ruffle shirts worn by maharajas. |
| 1974 | Modèle Trévise version (long necklace and pendant). |
| 1975 | Gazelle set. |
| 1976 | The ballet *Jewels* is presented at the Théâtre du Rond-Point des Champs-Elysées.<br>Lascaux set. |
| 1979 | Damiers set (Boutique). Palmyre set, gold net and diamonds. |
| 1980 | Squelette watch, which reveals its clockwork. |
| 1981 | Everest necklace. |
| 1982 | Mikado set. |
| 1983 | Lyre set. |
| 1985 | Or drapé and Mosaïque sets, inlay of hard stones and round diamonds. |
| 1990 | The Mystery Setting technique is perfected. |
| 1992 | The very first jewels in hexagonal Mystery Setting. |
| 2000 | Clip du Millénaire in the "Mysterious Setting".<br>Cadenas watch on leather strap and Cadenas necklace.<br>Zip necklace. |
| 2001 | Airelles necklace.<br>A new version of the Alhambra line.<br>Rings worn between the fingers. |
| 2002 | The Century collection of 523 coloured diamonds.<br>The Lotus line.<br>Cadenas watch on a golden bracelet.<br>Liberty brooch, Mystery set rubies.<br>Forêt ring, Mystery set rubies. |
| 2003 | The Romancing the Diamond Lines High Jewellery collection.<br>Songe d'une nuit d'été High Jewellery collection.<br>The Frivole line. |
| 2004 | The Couture High Jewellery collection.<br>The Hawaii line. |

## The History of a style

2004 A limited series of Papillons clips, decorated with motifs, by the master lacquerer Hakose-san.
The Chapeau Chinois line.

2005 The "Pierres de Caractère" High Jewellery collection.

2006 The "Une Journée à Paris" High Jewellery collection.
The "Trésors Révélés" High Jewellery collection. Unique pieces created using drawings selected from the Company archives, dating from 1920 to 1960.
The Magic Alhambra, Lucky Alhambra and Byzantine Alhambra collections.
Lady Arpels Dentelle watch, Lady Arpels Centenaire Poetic Complication watch, Monsieur Arpels Latérale watch.

2007 The Atlantide High Jewellery collection.
The "Ballet Précieux" collection, previewed in London during the staging celebrating the fortieth birthday of the ballet Jewels by the Royal Opera House.
The Sweet Alhambra line.
The Flowerlace line.
The Lady Arpels Papillon watches and Fleurette watches.
Féerie Poetic Complication watch.
Tourbillon movement and single dial watches.
Fox-trot High Jewellery watch.

2008 Les Audacieuses Connoisseur collection.
Les Jardins High Jewellery collection, previewed at the Château de Groussay, in Montfort l'Amaury.
Ligne Perlée by Van Cleef & Arpels.
Charms, Poetic Complication, Day/Night, Midnight in Paris watches and Timeless High Jewellery watches.

2009 Eternal Pearls Connoisseur collection.
Exclusive edition: Le Quattro Stagioni collection for the opening of the Milan boutique.
High Jewellery California Rêverie collection, previewed in Malibu, California.
High Jewellery 744 Fifth collection.
Papillons Connoisseur collection.
Une Journée à Paris Poetic Complication watch, Les Jardins extrordinary dial watches and High Jewellery Vicomte watch.

**The model Bettina**, in front of Van Cleef & Arpels's window display, Place Vendôme, circa 1953.
© Jean-Philippe Charbonnier/Top.

**Rose clip** comprising twenty-five petals made of rubies in Mystery Setting, two leaves made of emeralds in Mystery Setting, and veins in diamonds, gold and platinum setting, 614 rubies and 241 emeralds, 1938.
© Van Cleef & Arpels.

**The founding couple**: Estelle Arpels and Alfred Van Cleef, on their wedding day, 1896.
© Van Cleef & Arpels.

**Charles Arpels** in a calash at Place Vendôme, early twentieth century.
© Van Cleef & Arpels.

**Hélène Arpels** at the racetrack.
© Van Cleef & Arpels.

**Place Vendôme** lit up during the city of Paris's two thousandth anniversary celebration, 1951.
© Robert Doisneau/Rapho.

**The Van Cleef & Arpels boutique** in New York, 57th Street.
© Van Cleef & Arpels.

**Van Cleef & Arpels boutiques** (from left to right and from top to bottom) in Deauville, Beverly Hills, Cannes and Nice.
© Van Cleef & Arpels.

**Claude Arpels** opens the New York boutique in 1939. He develops the market in the United States, then in Japan. © Van Cleef & Arpels.
**Replica of the crown made for Farah Pahlavi's coronation** on October 25, 1967, exhibited in a window display at the Place Vendôme boutique.
© Van Cleef & Arpels.

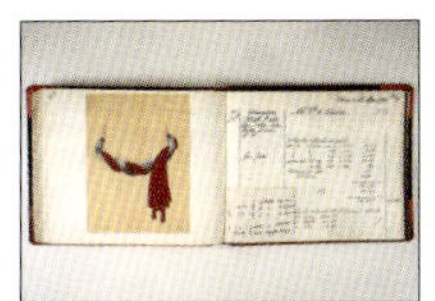

**Collerette diamond and ruby choker** made for the Duchess of Windsor. 1936 drawing extracted from order book and redrawn by René Sim Lacaze in 1939.
© Van Cleef & Arpels.

**The Duchess of Windsor** wearing the Collerette diamond and ruby choker made by René Sim Lacaze upon her request. Photo taken during a reception in New York, 1949. © All rights reserved.

**Grace Kelly** wearing the pearl and diamond necklace and earrings that Prince Rainier of Monaco gave her on the occasion of their engagement, 1956. Photography by Yousuf Karsh.
© The Estate of Yousuf Karsh/Camera Press.

The second wife of the Shah of Iran, **her Imperial Highness Soraya Esfandiari Bakhtiari**, wears Eventail earrings in platinum and diamonds, designed in 1951.
© All rights reserved.

**Minaudière** in engraved polished gold adorned with a pattern made of rubies in Mystery Setting, 1934.
© Van Cleef & Arpels.

**Van Cleef & Arpels workshops.**
© Masahiko Kishino/Van Cleef & Arpels.

**Van Cleef & Arpels workshops.**
© Masahiko Kishino / Van Cleef & Arpels.

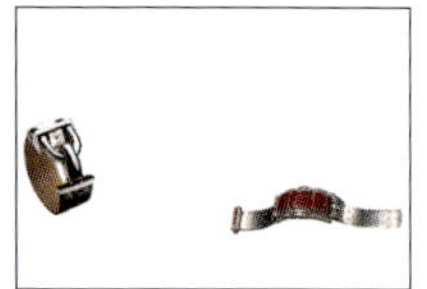

**Cadenas watch**, in steel on a satin bracelet. © Van Cleef & Arpels.
**Ludo bracelet** in platinum, round and baguette diamonds, the centre of which comprises three bands in Mystery set rubies, circa 1939. © Sotheby's.

**The maharajah of Rewa** wearing a diamond necklace made by Van Cleef & Arpels upon his request. © All Rights reserved.
**Indian fabric** with a floral pattern, sixteenth–seventeenth century. © Victoria and Albert Museum, London.

**Van Cleef & Arpels window display**, Place Vendôme. © All rights reserved.

**Cristaux de neige clip** in gold and diamonds. 1948. © Van Cleef & Arpels.
**Art deco vanity** made by Vladimir Makowsky, 1925. © Private collection, New York.
**Papillon ring** worn between the fingers, with diamonds and Mystery set sapphires. © Van Cleef & Arpels.

**Still life.** © Noëlle Hoppe, Bloom Magazine.
**Pavot Watch** made of rubies in Mystery Setting and diamonds set in gold. Band made of silk embroidery on duchess satin, 2000. © Van Cleef & Arpels.

**Diane Kruger** wears Lotus clips, together with the Nœud ring and bracelet, during the Une Journée à Paris event in 2006. © Olivier Borde

**Oiseaux de Paradis necklace** set in white, yellow and red gold, Mystery Set (TM) buff-top blue and mauve sapphires, pear-shaped blue and coloured 18.62 cts sapphires, calibrated emeralds and diamonds, 2009. © Yannick Le Merlus/Van Cleef and Arpels
**Ballerine clip** in diamonds, rubies and emeralds, 1941. © Van Cleef & Arpels.

**A seamstress on her way out of her workshop, Place Vendôme**, 1947. © Willy Ronis/Rapho.

**Bouquet Hawaii Trois clip.** Flowers in white gold, diamonds and aquamarines. © Van Cleef & Arpels.

**Jacqueline Kennedy** wearing two Van Cleef & Arpels Flamme brooches on her pearl necklace, 1962. © Marilyn Silverstone/Magnum photo.
**Bouquet brooch.** Flowers made of rubies in Mystery Setting and round diamonds for the centers, circa 1936. © California Collection.

**Oiseau du Paradis brooch**, feathers in sized sapphires and rubies, body in engraved polished gold, beak in round diamonds, and a cabachon ruby for the eye, 1942. Private collection.
© Van Cleef & Arpels.

**Lacquered Papillons clips**, decorated with motifs by the master lacquerer Hakose-san in a numbered limited edition. Papillons clips in gold and diamonds. © Van Cleef & Arpels.
**Midnight Extraordinary dial watch**, white gold case, Asian Garden dial, automatic movement, alligator strag. Dial in mother of pearl inlay and gold sculpting.
© Van Cleef & Arpels.

**Dentelle necklace** in white gold, diamonds, pink gold and pink diamonds, 2004. © Van Cleef & Arpels.

**Dentelle brooch** in pierced gold. Scalloped details and double knot in round diamonds set in platinum.
© Van Cleef & Arpels.
**Shawl**, Chantilly lace (bobbin lace, black silk), circa 1860.
Private collection. © All rights reserved.

**Zip necklace** in white gold, baguette diamonds and pear-shaped 14.22 ct diamond, collar in leather and embroidered silk, 2007.
© Van Cleef & Arpels.

**George Balanchine and Pierre Arpels with Suzanne Farrell** in the Place Vendôme salons, on the occasion of the performance of the ballet Jewels at the Champs Elysées Theatre, 1976. © All Rights reserved.
**Ballerine clip** in white gold, diamonds and colour diamonds.
© Yannick Le Merlus/Van Cleef & Arpels.

In 1973, after a recital at the Champs Elysées Theatre in Paris, **Maria Callas** signs autographs for her fans. She wears a 1967 Fleurs clip in faceted rubies and diamonds. © MARIA CALLAS and related rights™/© of the Estate of Maria Callas, used under license through Greenlight.

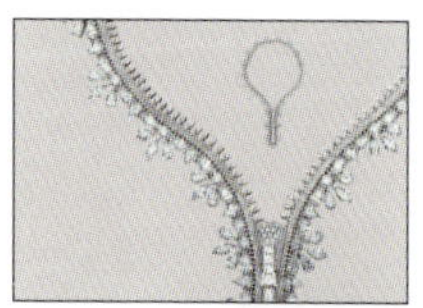

**Zip necklace** that can be worn as a bracelet, in white gold and diamonds, 2006. © Van Cleef & Arpels.

**Secret watch**, white gold case, black lacquer and diamonds, white mother-of-pearl face on a black satin strap, 2006.
© Van Cleef & Arpels.
**Caresse d'Eole necklace** in white gold and diamonds. The central motif can be removed and worn as a clip, 2004. © Van Cleef & Arpels.

**Farandole Necklace** in pear and navette diamonds, with two pear-shaped emeralds, 2001.
© Van Cleef & Arpels.

**Clip du Millénaire** in gold, platinum, rubies in Mystery Setting, round pear and baguette diamonds. The flower is detachable. 2000. Private collection.
© Van Cleef & Arpels.

At a party in 1951, **Marlene Dietrich** wears the famous Jarretière bracelet, set with cushion-cut rubies and diamonds. She also had worn it the previous year during the filming of Alfred Hitchcock's Stage Fright. A Christian Dior dress. © Deutsche Kinemathek/Marlene Dietrich Collection, Berlin. **Platinum Byzance solitaire**, set with diamonds and a cushion-cut 32.92 ct diamond, 2005. © Van Cleef & Arpels.

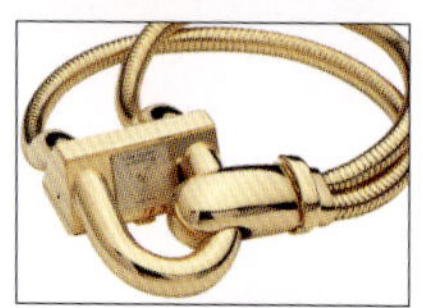

**Cadenas watch** on yellow gold serpent chain.
© Van Cleef & Arpels.

**Ruban Dentelle necklace** in white gold, diamonds and Mystery set rubies, 2005. © Van Cleef & Arpels.
**Flot de rubans** in diamonds on platinum. 1928.
© Van Cleef & Arpels.

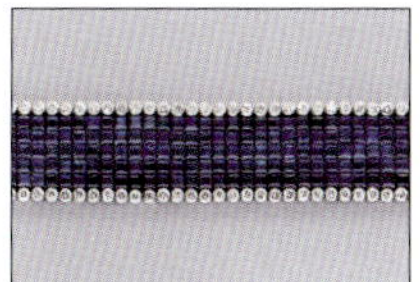

**Ruban bracelet** made of five rows of sapphires in Mystery Setting and diamonds, 1958.
© Van Cleef & Arpels.

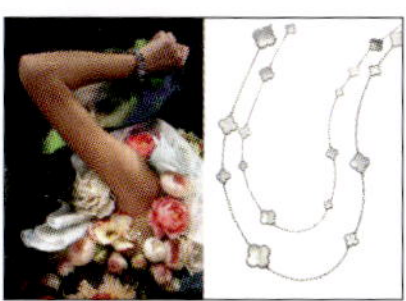

During **Viktor & Rolf**'s 2003 Spring-Summer fashion show, the models wore vintage jewels, such as a Feuillages bracelet made in 1939, in emeralds and sapphires on platinum. © Peter Stigter.
**Magic Alhambra long necklace,** in white gold, with chalcedony motifs and white and grey mother-of-pearl. © Yannick Le Merlus/Van Cleef & Arpels.

**The interior of the Van Cleef & Arpels boutique** on the Place Vendôme, decorated by Patrick Jouin for the centenary of the Maison, in 2006.
© Patricia Bailer / Van Cleef & Arpels.

© Lon van Keulen/*Bloom Magazine*.

The author especially wishes to thank:
Van Cleef & Arpels in Paris and New York, for its vigilant attention and desire to preserve a memory, particularly Isabelle Guichot, Ferdinand Garcia Ripoll, Shiryo Hayashi, Eric Jacolliot and their staff.
Eric Arpels for giving me access to a living memory.
Claude-Julien Arpels for locating the origins of the ballet *Jewels*.
Sylvie Raulet, the author of very rich monographs who remains the reference for any investigation on that subject, for sharing her profound and enthusiastic knowledge of Van Cleef & Arpels.
François Canavy.
Fabienne Faluel, curator at the Musée Galliéra.
Hubert Lebaudy for his talent in making images speak.
Claire Beaume, Laurence Caille and Eloïse Didier-Scapel.

Van Cleef & Arpels especially wishes to thank:
His Royal Majesty Prince Albert II of Monaco, Bettina Graziani, Diane Kruger and Viktor & Rolf.